Dirty Poem

NEW DIRECTIONS POETRY PAMPHLETS

#1 Susan Howe: *Sorting Facts; or, Nineteen Ways of Looking at Marker*

#2 Lydia Davis / Eliot Weinberger: *Two American Scenes*

#3 Bernadette Mayer: *The Helens of Troy, NY*

#4 Sylvia Legris: *Pneumatic Antiphonal*

#5 Nathaniel Tarn: *The Beautiful Contradictions*

#6 Alejandra Pizarnik: *A Musical Hell*

#7 H.D.: *Vale Ave*

#8 Forrest Gander: *Eiko & Koma*

#9 Lawrence Ferlinghetti: *Blasts Cries Laughter*

#10 Osama Alomar: *Fullblood Arabian*

#11 Oliverio Girondo: *Poems to Read on a Streetcar*

#12 *Fifteen Iraqi Poets* (ed., Dunya Mikhail)

#13 Anne Carson: *The Albertine Workout*

#14 Li Shangyin: *Derangements of My Contemporaries*

#15 Sakutarō Hagiwara: *The Iceland*

#16 *Poems of Osip Mandelstam* (ed., Peter France)

#17 Robert Lax: *Hermit's Guide to Home Economics*

#18 Ferreira Gullar: *Dirty Poem*

#19 Amelia Rosselli: *Hospital Series*

Dirty Poem

FERREIRA GULLAR

Translated from the Portuguese by Leland Guyer

NEW DIRECTIONS POETRY PAMPHLET #18

This translation was first published by the University Press of America in 1990 and then later
in the anthology *Ferreira Gullar: An Ordinary Man*, published by Colección Patricia Phelps de
Cisneros in 2013. It has been substantially revised for this edition.

Cover design by Erik Carter
Interior design by Eileen Krywinski and Erik Rieselbach
Manufactured in the United States of America
New Directions Books are printed on acid-free paper.
First published as New Directions Poetry Pamphlet #18 in 2015

Library of Congress Cataloging-in-Publication Data
Gullar, Ferreira, 1930–
[Poema sujo. English]
Dirty poem / Ferreira Gullar; translated by Leland Guyer.
pages cm
ISBN 978-0-8112-2395-9 (alk. paper)
I. Guyer, Leland, translator. II. Title.
PQ9698.17.U53P613 2015
869.1'42— dc23   2014032855

10 9 8 7 6 5 4 3 2 1

ndbooks.com

New Directions Books are published for James Laughlin
by New Directions Publishing Corporation
80 Eighth Avenue, New York 10011

PREFACE

Wander here
Wander there
Work is done, get out of town
The city isn't in me now
—*Chico Buarque*

———————

The man is in the city
as a thing is in another city
and the city is in the man
who is in another city
—*Ferreira Gullar*

Ferreira Gullar wrote *Poema Sujo*, or *Dirty Poem*, in 1975 while in exile in Buenos Aires, Argentina. It is largely a meditation on growing up in a French-Portuguese colonial city on the northeastern Brazilian coast. It begins at a level of childish consciousness; moves on to explore his evolution of personal identity through a wide range of experiences that include sex, travel, and poetry; and concludes with a clearly defined revelation that social and political justice are unrealized. All of this he ponders poetically while living in political exile.

It is hard to appreciate the poem without knowing that the history of the Brazilian Northeast is marked by mass migrations from the semiarid and near-feudal lands and mostly impoverished towns to the industrialized cities of the South. A sense of migrant dislocation is evoked in the first epigraph above, taken from Chico Buarque's song "Assentamento" (Settlement). Disillusioned and dejected, the immigrant pronounces that "The city isn't in me now," and longs to return to the land that had once driven him away. The second epigraph, from the concluding verses of *Dirty Poem*, expresses a similar but different relationship with the city when, unable to return home, he laments that "the city is in the man / who is in another city." Like Buarque's migrant persona, Gullar fled the endemically poor Northeast but retains a similar rootedness to the area.

Ferreira Gullar was born in 1930 in equatorial São Luís, the capital of the state of Maranhão. A primary subject of the poem, São Luís is a stunning, if decaying, island city of colonial architecture that lies in the estuary formed by several rivers that empty into the Atlantic. The city was a distant outpost in the seventeenth century when it was founded, and it remains relatively isolated even today.

The adolescent Gullar gained his formal education at a trade school, but he soon realized that art, literature, and philosophy attracted him more, and so educated himself with the relatively few books to which he had access. His early years impressed upon him the value of poetry's utility, a theme that would mark some of the most significant points in his aesthetic trajectory. Growing up in São Luís, however, imposed irreconcilable limitations on Gullar's aspirations as a writer.

He left the city to work as a journalist in Rio de Janeiro in the early 1950s, and his reputation as an experimental poet attracted the attention of the "Concrete" writers associated with the Noigandres group in São Paulo. Because this group had tired of traditional poetic forms, they explored verse characterized by extreme rationalized geometrics, influenced by other experimental poets such as e.e. cummings, Ezra Pound, and Dylan Thomas. Gullar initially found the group interesting but the Concrete poets were too socially and politically aloof for his taste, and he and a number of other writers and artists founded the polemical splinter Neo-Concrete arts movement. A primary goal of this group was to depart from the strictures of the Concretists and introduce a more human and less mechanistic dimension into the practice of poetry and the plastic arts.

Ultimately, Gullar's dedication to the avant-garde abated, and in 1962 he joined one of the Peoples' Culture Centers—leftist student organizations engaged in making the arts more accessible to the masses. He hoped that this environment would enable him to respond more directly to his persistent concern that art have a clear social meaning and utility. This experience did not last long, however, as in 1964 eroding political, economic, and social conditions led to a military coup that would hold repressive dictatorial power until 1985. Any art considered radical in form or content was suspect, and anyone with the hint of a Socialist or Communist affiliation became an immediate target. Gullar represented both camps.

During the military dictatorship Gullar endured harassment and arrest by the military police who had begun to detain, torture, and "disappear" political undesirables. He feared for his life, went into hiding, and in 1971 fled the country and traveled from Buenos Aires to Paris and Moscow and then to Santiago, Chile. He arrived in Santiago just in time to witness the bloody 1973 coup that overthrew the Socialist government of Salvador Allende. Gullar slipped through a lethal dragnet and fled the country, going first to Buenos Aires, then to Lima, and back to Buenos Aires.

Unfortunately Argentina was no friendlier to him than either Brazil or Chile. He was separated from his family, he feared Brazilian operatives in Argentina, his passport had expired, and leaving the country had become impossible. All he had left was his poetry and it was to his poetry that he would turn. Terrified that he would soon be apprehended, he decided to write "a last will and testament" that would recover a part of his past in a variety of poetic forms that shaped his aesthetic journey:

I felt that I could die at any moment and that I had to write a poem that would say it all, that would bring some resolution to my life, that would leave nothing unsaid, that would be my last will and testament.... And, at the same time, the poem would be my way of clinging to life and to joy and to create a new foundation I could stand on. I was devastated, and perhaps for this reason I chose to return to São Luís, to my childhood, to those happy days, which although not always so happy, were days that my memories clung to.

I had tried to write about my life in São Luís before, to write about its people and its universe and their relation to the problem of time, to the problem of the mortality of things, those things that end but remain within us. I wanted to recover a life long past to demonstrate that what had died was actually still alive. But it was more than just a return to the past, not an escape but a bringing forth of the past into the present. And so there is a mystery between time and space—a relationship that had bothered me from the very beginning—that is made manifest through *Dirty Poem*. I sought a non-metaphysical profundity, the essence of concrete reality.

Dirty Poem transcends itself through the relationships things have with one another. For instance, the pear connects with the living room, which in turn connects with certain individuals, who in turn connect with the city, which connects with the entire world beyond it. And the pear also works its chemical processes internally. It has sugars, alcohols; it has its own death processes, amid whose work emerges something new. This is what fascinates me—the complexity of the real, the reality of things and their concrete, non-metaphysical existence.

Gullar's poem is about exile, as well as the city "in the man /
who is in another city." It is about the consolation and the power of
memory, even if memory is "dirty." Perhaps *especially* if it is dirty,
because life is dirty. Dirty in this poem includes memories of sexual
encounters, but also the outrage of social and physical decay, poverty,
hopelessness, corruption, and oppression in all its guises. While these
motifs may be unsettling, the facts of human interchange, organic
decomposition, and even social injustices are, of course, real, as are
the possibilities of birth and rebirth. Gullar's profound optimism
glimmers through the corruption in passages of glowing beauty,
lyrical rhythms, and moments of great tenderness. The scholar and
critic Otto Maria Carpeaux put it succinctly when he wrote, "Ferreira
Gullar is one of the greatest men of our country [and] *Dirty Poem*
should be called *National Poem*, as it embodies all of the experiences,
victories, defeats, and hopes of Brazilian life."

LELAND GUYER

SOURCES

Buarque, Chico, "Assentamento." In Sebastião Salgado, *Terra*,
   introduction by José Saramago. São Paulo: Companhia
   das Letras, 1997.

Carpeaux, Otto Maria. In Ferreira Gullar, *Poema Sujo*, fifth
   edition. Rio de Janeiro: Editora Civilização Brasileira, 1983.

Gullar, Ferreira. *Toda Poesia (1950–1999)*, ninth edition, preface by
   Sérgio Buarque de Holanda. São Paulo: José Olympio
   Editora, 2000.

Guyer, Leland. "Exile and the Sense of Place in Ferreira Gullar's
   Dirty Poem." *Macalester International. Landscape, Culture, and
   Globalization: Views from Brazil*, 5 (1997), 180–91.

———— "An Interview with Ferreira Gullar." *Discurso Literario* 5
   (1987), 26–41.

Dirty Poem

DIRTY POEM

muddy muddy
the muddy
hand of the wind
against the wall
dull
less less
less than dull
less than soft and solid less than a well and a wall: less than a hollow
dull
more than dull
bright
like water? like a plume? bright more than bright right: nothing at all
and all
(or nearly all)
a creature conceived by the universe has been dreaming from its belly
blue
the cat was
blue
the cock was
blue
the colt was
blue
your ass

your gums like your little pussy that seemed to smile among the
banana leaves flowery perfumes swine shit open like a body's
mouth (unlike your speaking mouth) like an opening to
I didn't know you
didn't know how

to make life spin
with its mass of stars and ocean
entering us in you

lovely lovely
more than lovely
but what was her name?
It wasn't Helena or Vera
or Nara or Gabriela
or Tereza or Maria
Her name her name was . . .
It vanished in her frigid flesh
it vanished in the confusion of so many nights and days
it vanished in the profusion of things and their ways
    alphabet constellations
    nights composed in chalk
    birthday candies
    soccer Sundays
    burials processions rallies
    roulette billiards cards
she changed her face and hair she changed her eyes and smiles she
changed her home and time: but she is with me
    your name is
    lost within me
    in some drawer

What does a name matter at this hour of the evening in São Luís do
Maranhão at the dining table beneath a fevered lamp among brothers
and sisters
and parents within an enigma?
                    but what does a name matter

beneath this roof of grimy tiles open beams among
chairs and a table between a china cabinet and a cupboard among
knives and forks and broken plates

        a plate of simple fired clay doesn't endure

        and the knives are lost and the forks

        are lost in their lifetime they fall

        through the cracks between floorboards and mingle

with the rats
and roaches or rust in the backyard forgotten among the stalks of
ginger grass
and the thick mint leaves

        so many things are lost

        in this life

        Just like what they said was lost right there

        chewing

        mixing beans with manioc and chunks of roasted meat

and they said things just as real as the embroidered tablecloth
or auntie's cough in the bedroom
and the sunbeam dying on the frieze that faced our
our window

        so real that

        they were extinguished forever

                Or were they?

I don't know the fabric of my flesh and this dizziness
that drags me through the avenues and vaginas among the smells
of gas and piss consuming me like a flameless torch-body,

        or inside a bus

        or in the belly of a Boeing 707 above the Atlantic

above the rainbow

                    perfectly beyond
                    chronological rigor
                    dreaming
Rusted forks dull knives ragged chairs and worn-out tables
grocery counters Alegria Street paving stones eaves of houses
shrouded with mold mossy walls words said at the dining-room
table,
                    you fly with me
                    over continents and seas
And you crawl with me too
                    through the tunnels of clandestine nights
                    beneath the nation's starry sky
                    among the splendor and the leprosy
between the sheets of mud and dread
                    you slip away with me, old tables,
antiquated cupboards perfumed drawers of the past,
                    you turn the corners of terror with me
                    and you wait you wait
for the day to come

                    And in the end
                    what does a name matter?
I cover you with flowers, sweetie, and I give you each and every name;
                    I call you dawn
                    I call you water
I discover you in colored stones in movie stars
                    in the visions of my dreams

                    —And that woman coughing in the house!
As if the poverty, the dim lamp, the cheap perfume,
the meager love, the leaky winter roof were not enough.
And the ants surging by the millions gushing black from

within the walls (as if the essence of the house)
And all were seeking

> in a smile in a gesture
> in corner conversations
> in sex while standing on the darkened Quartel
> promenade
> in adultery
> in robbery
> the solution to the riddle

> —What shall I do in the meantime?
> —From what shall I defend myself?

In the backyard herbs and roses grew in a creel left in the black dirt
> (how can perfume
> come from that?)

In the mud along the sidewalks, from the sewer water grew
tomato plants
On the tiles of the eaves of the homes grew grass
> greener than hope
> (or the fire
> of your eyes)
It was life exploding through all the city's cracks
in the shadows of the war:

> the gestapo wehrmacht raf feb blitzkrieg
catalinas torpedoing the fifth column fascists nazis communists the
esso newsman on the radio quarrels in the grocery kerosene andiroba
nut soap the black market rationing the blackout mountains of scrap
metal the italian assassinated in João Lisboa Plaza the scent of gun-
powder the german cannons thundering in the stormy nights above
our house. Stalingrad resists. For my father who smuggled cigarettes,

for my cousin who sold lotto tickets, for my uncle who stole tin from the Railroad, for Senhor Neco who rolled cheap cigars, for Sergeant Gonzaga who drank manioc brandy with honey and fucked with the window wide open,

> for my docile lamb
> for my blue city
> for Brazil, hail hail,

Stalingrad resists.
To each new morning
in the windows on the corners in the headlines

But poetry didn't yet exist.

> Flora. Fauna. Odors. Dresses.
> Tits. Eyes. Biceps. Faces.
> Green glass, jasmine.
> Bikes on Sunday.
> Kites of paper.
> Bandstand concerts in the plaza.
> Mourning.
> Dead man in the market,
> his blood on the vegetables.
> Voiceless world, opaque thing.

Neither Olavo Bilac nor Raimundo Correia. Blatant tuba, artless lyre? Neither tuba nor Grecian lyre. I learned later: human speech, people's voices, dark sounds of the body, bracketed by lightning.

> The body. But what is the body?
> My body of flesh and blood.
> Invisible bones, jawbones, ribs,
> > flexible framework that suspends me in space

          that keeps me from collapsing like an empty
          sack
       that keeps all my organs
              working
       like tubes and retorts
       making the blood that makes my flesh and thoughts
         and words
         and lies
and the sweetest horniest
         caresses
poised to burst like a galaxy
         of milk
       between your thighs in the depths
       of your avid night
the scents of navel and vagina
         grave indecipherable smells
         like symbols
         of the body
of your body of my body
body
that a sword can cut
         a splinter of broken glass
         a razor
my body brimming with blood
         that waters it like a continent
         or a garden
         coursing through my arms
         through my fingers
         while I quarrel I walk
         I remember I recall
my blood comprised of the gases I breathe

of these foreign city airs
with the help of the sycamores
can—with a bit of inattention—slip through my
opened
wrist
My body
I see stretched upon the bed
like an object in space
that measures five feet six
and it is I: that thing
stretched out
belly legs feet
each with five toes (why
not six?)
knees and ankles
for moving about
sitting down
getting up

my 5' 6" body which is my size in this world
my body made of water
and ashes
makes me gaze at Andromeda, Sirius, Mercury
and makes me feel a part of
all that mass of hydrogen and helium
disintegrating and reintegrating
with no one knowing why

Body, my body body
that has a nose and a mouth as well
as two eyes
and a special way of smiling

of speaking
that my mother identifies as being of her son
        that my son identifies
        as being of his father
body which if it ceases to function provokes
        a profound stir in the family:
        without it José Ribamar Ferreira ceases to exist
        Ferreira Gullar is no more
and many small events on earth
will forever be forgotten

body-flame   body-fool   body-fact

pierced by smells of chicken coops and rats
in the grocery nest
        of rats
        the shit of cats
salt verdigris spats
        cheap ring brilliantine
analingus cunnilingus genital warts crab lice
        in pubic hair
body my body-phallus
        unfathomable uncomprehended
my domestic dog my owner
        sated with dreams and flowers
my body-galaxy open to everything full
        of everything like a trash heap
of filthy rags old cans used mattresses symphonies
        sambas and frevos blues
        by Fra Angelico greens
        by Cézanne
        dream-matter by Volpi

But above all my
                    northeastern
                    body
          more than this
                    maranhanian
more than this
                    sanluisian
          more than this
                    ferreirian
                    newtonian
                    alzirian
my body born in a one-door-and-a-window house on Prazeres Street
                    neighbor to a bakery
                    under the sign of Virgo
                    under the shells of the Twenty-fourth Cavalry
                    during the Revolution of 1930
and which since then keeps beating like a clock
                    with a tick tock you cannot hear
(unless you press your ear to my heart)
                    tick tock tick tock
while I stroll among buses and cars
                    past fashion windows
                    in the bookstores
                    in the bars
                    tick tock tick tock
beating now for forty-five years
                    this hidden heart
beating in the middle of the night, in the snow, in the rain
under my cape, my jacket, my shirt,
under my skin, my flesh,
clandestine combatant on the side of the working class
                    my childish heart

                              bright bright
                              more than just bright
                                                  white
the lightning illuminates continents past:
                                        night and jasmine
                                        next to the house

voices lost in the mud
empty Sundays

                              water dreaming in the barrel
nation of brush and rust

                              scrabbling for copper and aluminum
                              in unplowed lands
                              wartime economy?
                              for me just
                              cracklings and movies

Alone at that
river estuary
                              beneath the hot tropical sun
alone in the afternoon on the planet in history
                              hauling around shrimp
                              in a straw basket
                                        what was I
looking for there?
                              Was the Trojan War ever fought?
                              Homer Dante Boccaccio?
                              When did geometry appear?

Just mud and salt water
just catfish and puffers
sand wind sun and rain
and the colored sails
of the boats on the bay:
                              what did I question there
with that basket in my hands
beneath the sun of Maranhão?
It wasn't the sun of Laplace,
nor was it the geographic island:
                                        it was the sun
                                        just the sun
                                        with the scent of rotting mud
                                        and the odor of fish and people
                                        corvina bonito dogfish

          catfish eating shit
             at the outflow of the sewer
land of salt and rust
             what was I looking for there
walking the rails
                    bemused
          hopping from tie to tie
          wandering the smooth mud
banks toads bottles
          full of mud, pipes
where the shoal fish lived
                              walking
aimlessly among railway cars
          wheels leprous axels
          abandoned
bearing races packed
          with dirt rust grease
          grass covered with oil

What did those classes teach me
        in solitude
        among the things of nature
and of man?
                The tall zinc shed
shimmers of solder
                workers in the shade
walls blackened from smoke
It wasn't a house: a house
has chairs tables armchairs
                Perhaps
it was a temple? but
with no niches no altar no saints?

What was it, a factory?

                        where with grinding wheel sparks
the afternoon grew hot as a forge
where the afternoon was another
afternoon
that had nothing to do with the one
I now saw in the distance
        beyond the railway
        beyond the docks
        beyond the waters of the Anil, there
        blinded by the sun behind the ruins
        of the Ponta d'Areia Fort
        at the entrance to the bay

How many afternoons rolled into one!
        and it was another, a cool one,
an afternoon under the good trees
on Jenipapeiro beach

Or from the other side the
still grander city afternoon
   heaped with apartments and belvederes
   steep streets backyards grocery shops
   gardens stilt houses chicken coops
or in the (distant) kitchen where Bizuza
   prepares the dinner
       and doesn't sing

   oh how many rolled into one
inclusive afternoon that covers the city with clouds
   weaving above us and with us
   the blank history
   of any small life

oh winds blowing green in the palms of Remédios Plaza
grass growing dark beneath my feet
   between the rails
and within the afternoon the locomotive-
   afternoon
that approaches like a steel
   pachyderm
   overdue and heavy
jaw clenched head hissing
   a cathedral in motion
   enveloped in steam
   puffing panic
      ready
   to explode

chi chi
   chu chu chu

choo CHOO CHOO
     chi chi chi chi chi
CHOO CHOO CHOO CHOO CHOO CHOO

*(To be sung to the music of the second
Bachiana from Villa-Lobos' Tocata)*

there goes the train with the boy
there goes life on its way
there go the dance and destiny
city and night in a spin
there goes the rambling train
looking for the morning light
speeding over land

        it passes through the mountains
        it passes by the sea
    chanting through mountains of moonlight
    rumbling past the stars

                wide and far

    wheeee-ee! whee-ee whee-ee

                wide and far

    whee-ee whee-ee whee-ee

    goodbye classmates
    goodbye hook and bait
    goodbye girl I tried to mate
    the train has me aboard and will not hesitate

OO-OO   OO-OO OO-OO OO-OO
       ca-chug ca-chug ca-chug

breezes clear and breezes keen
almost day this grayish scene

OO-EE OO-EE OO-EE OO-EE OO-EE
ca-chug   ca-chug   ca-chug

baboom baboom bababoom
baboom baboom bababoom
baboom baboom bababoom
baboom baboom bababoom baboom bababoom baboom bababoom
baboom baboom baboom
baboom baboom baboom

OO-EE OO-EE OO-EE OO-EE OO-EE
oo-ee oo   oo-ee oo-ee oo-ee oo-ee oo-ee

we left home at four
streetlights still ablaze

Father carried a small suitcase
I just had a bag

we walked toward Afogados
up streets and other stairs

for him it was routine
for me it was a thrill

when we got to the station
the train was waiting there

there at rest and ready
very long and whistling

we got on board the car
I was both glad and afraid

my father (dead and gone)
kept me by his side

perhaps more happy than I
for taking me along

my father (dead and gone)
smiled with sparkling eyes

OO-OO   OO-OO OO-OO OO-OO

    chug chug chug
    chug chug chug

CA-CHOO CA-CHOO CA-CHOO
CA-CHOO CA-CHOO CA-CHOO

    we overtook the night
    as we passed through Perizes
    which was precisely where
    the day began

OO-OO OO-OO OO-OO
OO-OO OO-OO OO-OO

    and seeing all the life
    spread out in open fields
    and the ducks and oxen
    living unattached to me
    and all the trees and water

clouds and grasses—how
small the city seemed!

And oh the world was large:
the train had rolled for hours
and never reached the end
of all that sky of all that land
of all those fields and mountains
not counting Piauí

We passed through Rosário
through Vale-Quem-Tem, Quelru.
We passed through Pirapemas
and through Itapicuru:
world of oxen, crested cranes,
titmice, ducks, and tinamous

bread and coffee
              tea cake no
                            bread and coffee
                                          tea cake no
value makes the man
                    value makes the man
                                      value makes the man
        value makes the man
                  there's no value
in just the man
                nothing is of value
there's no
          value
in the man
            in this valley

there's no
value
there's no
value
for the man who
has
no
value
in the
v
a
l
l
e
y

        HISSSSS!!!

                    Many
there are many days in one
                              for things themselves
comprise them
with their flesh (or iron or
                         whatever name
time-matter goes by
                         dirty or
                         not)
                                   comprise them
in their explicit or heavy silences
like flannel quilts
or dizzily still waters
                    as
on the Medeiros' farm, in their
farm well
                    covered by the near panicked shadows
                              of the trees
                    of the branches that climbed silently
                              like enigmas
                              completely still
like a green or vegetal and watery
                              night
although up in the trees
                         on top
                         way up high
dripping down their luminous flanks in their leaves
                              the day passed (the twentieth
                              century)
                    and it was day
as it was day that
                         day

in our living room

the table with its cloth the chairs the

wooden floor worn to a shine

and the bright smile on Lucinha rocking in the hammock

with death already poised

at her throat

without anyone knowing

—and it doesn't matter—

I leaned on the porch rail

saw the dark earth of the backyard

and the chicken scratching and pecking at

a cockroach among the plants

and in this case a double-day

inside and outside

of the living room

one at my back the other

before my eyes

ebbing one into the other

through my body

days both now ebbing in the very heart

of Buenos Aires

at four in the afternoon

May 22, 1975

thirty years later

many

many are the days in one

easy to understand

but difficult to penetrate

to the core of each of those many days

because they're more than they seem

since

there are other days
or there were
on that day of the well
at the farm
inside and outside too
because it isn't possible to separate
one from the other
those days of impalpable edges
made of—say—fruits and leaves
fruits which in themselves are
a day
of sugar forming in the pulp
or opening onto other surrounding
days
like a horizon of endless works:

because a few steps
from the well
up from the earthen steps
on the treeless street
where I just walked
pass people and wagons
or someone shouts from the window
while a bird flies (possi-
bly)
over us
a vulture perhaps
soaring toward Camboa
leisurely over the vast pasture and beyond the railroad
above the thatched huts in the mud
and beyond the factory
built on a slab emitting a plume of ashes and cotton
dust

a vulture
himself a black day sniffing rotting meat
        and in the rotting meat
next to the Slaughterhouse
           stinking
      the day (a day) rots
               surrounding the day
      of the mudflat slum dwellers
      and the day of the vulture
      and the day of the Sol Levante olive oil can
      which resting on three stones
      on the thatched hut's beaten earth floor
where Esmagado lives
        boils
        bacon and rice
     for his lunch
and all these days linked like smoke rings
      encircling the weather vane
      disintegrating in the clouds
and the clamor of the tanagers among the sapodilla trees
        at six in the afternoon
        or
     in the bucket of shade and vertigo
        of the water
        in the well
on the farm
     the years have left behind

     And they retrieve more and more
     sounding an alarm in my flesh
     the silence of that water
     its shadow

a glimmer
under my nails
as then beneath the leaves full of sugar and light
dripping with water
a chirp
a breath of wind
unhurried
and everywhere
the night would build itself
poison us with jasmine

And later the night would swiftly tumble down
with its dark carriage
banging iron
like a train
through Costela do Diabo
with its parade of bats
You couldn't discern
with so few lights
the nature of its horses
its driver his whip
galloping through my dream
with no brothers to witness

In a single night there are many nights
but different
from how there are days
in one day
(especially in the neighborhoods
where there's so little light)
because at night
all our certainties grow dim

and nature closes

her colorful eyes

hides her creatures

between her thighs, places her birds among her fruits

and calms all waters

though she continues to pee

hidden

in places on the farm

so softly that almost no one beneath the arum leaves can hear her

And in this way many nights

seem only one

or two at most:

the other being

the night inside the house

lit by bulbs

Night puts the hens to sleep

sets to work the movie houses

activates

the radio shows, provokes

quarrels at the dinner table, excesses

in youngsters who kiss and pet

next to the gate

in the darkness

and when the tension becomes too great they

decide to marry

(except, for example,

Maria do Carmo

who let the soldiers

suck her prodigious breasts

on Silva Maia Avenue

beneath the oitizeiro trees

and let them come
between her hot thighs—without
penetration—
and who returned home
hating her father
and dissatisfied with life)

At night, since
there's so little light,
we're under the impression
that time doesn't pass

or at least it doesn't flow
as it flows by day:
like an interruption
for Dr. Bacelar to make a speech
at the Portuguese Literary Recreation Society
an interruption
so that the workers of the Camboa factory
can rest a little
and couple in their hammocks
or on their mats
making love quietly
to avoid waking the children asleep in the same room

As if time
during the night
had stopped along
with the darkness and the dust
beneath the furniture and
in the corners of the house
(even inside
the wardrobe,

time,
        hung on hangers)
        And this sensation
is even more vivid
                when we wake up late
                and everything is bright
                and already running: birds
trees vegetable vendors

        Or when
we wake up early and stay
                in bed musing through
                the early-morning process:
                the first steps in the street
                                        the first
                sounds in the kitchen
                                        until from rooster to rooster
                a nearby
                rooster
                erupts
                (in the backyard)
                and the tap of the laundry tub
                opens to gush the morning

        Night makes us believe
(given the little light)
                that time is an audible
                entity.
                After the nighttime chores
                (which filled the house with sounds
                including the last small talk in bed)
                when the whole family is finally asleep

time becomes a purely
chemical phenomenon
and doesn't disrupt
                        (rather
lulls)
            our sleep.

        And yet,
    someone who comes in from the street
—having traveled beneath the frightening stillness
        of the Milky Way—
                            could presume
        from those sleeping bodies
                        that the universe has died
                        when in fact
                        from all the city's faucets
                        morning is set to gush

        Except, of course,
in the Baixinha mudflat slum, along
the railroad,
            where there is no running water:
            there
            the gleam contained beneath the night
            is not
            as it is in the city
            water's fist clenched within the pipes:
            it is life's
            fist
            clenched within the mud

There it is clear
that night isn't the same
        in every part of the city;
        in Baixinha
        night doesn't have
        the same stillness
because the lamplight
        doesn't mesmerize
        as electricity can
mesmerize:
although time doesn't flow here either,
neither does it surge: it flickers
                it wavers
        in a cage of shadows.

But what separates
this Baixinha night most
        from the others
        is the aroma: rather
        the foul odor
it shares with the muddy flesh
        of certain animals

and for this reason you can say
        that the Baixinha night
doesn't pass, it doesn't
        flow:
                it rots

In something that rots
—let's take an old example:
                a pear—

time
doesn't flow or wail,
                                instead
                it sinks into its own abyss,
                                        it becomes lost
                in its own vortex
                                but so slowly
                that instead of turning to light it turns to
                darkness
                                rotting is
                                in fact the fabrication
                                of a night:
                                                whether
                                a pear on a plate or
                                a river in a working-class neighborhood

                                That is why in Baixinha
there are two nights one within the other: the suburban
night (with no running
                water) that dissolves when exposed to the sun
                                        and the subhuman night
                                        of mud
                                        that remains
                                        throughout the day
                                        spread
                                        like grease
                                        along stretches of mangrove

the deep night
of sleep (when
the workers dream)
and the shallow night
of mud beneath
the house

42

a night within another
like the tongue in the mouth
I might say
like a dresser
drawer (lower
still: the pecker in the pussy)
or like unused
black clothes inside the drawer
or some dirty thing
(a sense of guilt)
within a person
or even like
a drawer of mud
in a dresser of mud,
                              and so
perhaps the Baixinha night was a
crowned black princess
rotting in the mangroves

But to define this Baixina night
better
                              one should not separate it
from those who live there
                              —for the night is not
just
the conspiracy of things—
nor should one separate it from the
factory of thread and striped cloth
(which men make into pants)
where those people work,
nor from those people who don't make
even the minimum wage,

nor should one separate the mud
factory from the thread
factory
nor the thread
from the stinking air
poisoned by the mud
which from stinking for so many years
is now part of those people
                              (as
the scent of an animal can be part
of another animal)
                    and to such a degree
that no one can
recall any flower without
a stench of muddy sourness
(and they love each other
anyway)

It remains to say
—in order to understand
this proletarian night—
that a river doesn't rot as
a pear does
not only because a river doesn't rot on a plate
        but because nothing rots
        like something else
                        (or for it)
                          so even

a banana
doesn't rot like
a bunch of bananas
inside
a barrel

   —in a room of a house
    on Hortas Street, a mother
    ironing clothes—
making vinegar
    —as the Gonçalves Dias streetcar
    rolled down Rio Branco Street
    toward Remédios Plaza and other
    streetcars ran along Paz Street
    toward João Lisboa Plaza
    and still others would run
    toward Fabril, Apeadouro,
    Jordoa
    (this one was the Anil streetcar
    that took us
    to swim in the Azul River)
and the bananas
fermenting
working for their owner—as Marx would say—
hour after hour but with a rhythm
different (much
    thicker) from the clock
turning to vinegar
    —in the room where the whole family
    slept and
    sold pumpkins and okra—
fermenting
    —while Josias, the nurse,
    practiced medicine in my father's
    grocery store
      and I hid
    and played pool
    in Constâncio's bar

                    by the Ribeirão Fountain—
                                                but

a river
doesn't make vinegar
                    the way food rots when the grocer stores it
in a barrel
a river
doesn't rot as bananas rot
            not even, for example, as
            a woman's leg rots
                            —(the woman
            no one saw
            but who stank all morning
            in the house next to our school,
                                    during
                                    the war)
a river doesn't rot like a leg rots
            —although they both end up
            with bluish skin—
            not even as a garden rots
            (at least in our city
            beneath the lingering summer lightning)

            And as no river rots
            like another river
            the Anil river
            rotted in its own way
            on its part of the São Luís Island.
            Precisely because
            for another river
            to rot like this one
            it would have to run

along the same path
through the slaughterhouse
and mix its own river smell with the smell
of rotting meat
a cloud of vultures
forever hovering above it
as the Anil flows before
winding to the left
and losing itself in the sea
                              (in fact

drowning itself, writhing
into the salty waters
of the bay
that mingle with it, through its veins,
through its sweet river flesh
that pushes it back
muddles it
poisons it with salt
and makes it rot
                    —now that it cannot flow—
beneath the mudflat slums
where the workers from the Camboa
Textiles Factory live)

This is how the Anil rots
to the east of our city
which the French founded in 1612
which they found already rotting
although with a smell
that bears no relation
to the oil of the ships entering

the port almost daily now
        nor to the shit the city
        empties into its body of fishes
        nor to the misery of men
        slaves to others
        who live there
        like crabs today

        Only the Timbira Indians came to bathe
at Jenipapeiro beach, only they
        heard the wind in the trees
        and walked where
        today are streets and avenues,
mud-stained homes
        full of hammocks and memories
        in the darkness

        But nothing remains of those
Timbiras, except stories told in books
        and some poems that try
to evoke the shadows of the warriors
        hidden among the leaves
        with their bows
        (which doesn't stop a child
        having seen *Y Juca Pyrama*
        in the school theater
                from setting out in search
        of those people
        —his heart pounding—
        in the forests of Maioba or Jordoa
        but he finds only
        the sound of wind in the trees)

Unless he sees
a red-and-blue bird
perched in the leaves
—the breeze spreading its feathers like
a fan like
the plume of a warrior
who became that bird
to continue living in the forest
And even if
the bird is not the warrior
it was, no doubt, watched by him
and therefore
strangely
he is present there
watching it again
maybe now just behind the child just behind
the branches
when
something stirs
and a lizard flashes across the dry leaves

And all this happens
beneath the canopy of trees
(far
from the road that streetcars and buses
travel,
and farther still
from the streets of Praia Grande
clogged with trucks
street vendors like João Coelho and stevedores
unloading palm oil kernels)
all this happens

as part of the history of the forests and the birds
> And in the history of the birds
> the warriors live.

Before I had never thought
there was a history of birds
although I'd come to know so many birds

> > > from

the yellow finch (in Senhor Neco's
cage) to the dove
(on the roof ridge),

> > even the finch
(that was snared in the pasture),
> > > the red-cowled cardinal
> > > looked like an officer
> > > in full dress,
> > > the cuckoo was a worker
> > > for public sanitation,
> > > the vulture, a black man
> > > in a morning coat, the tyrant flycatcher,
> > > a policeman with a whistle in his mouth
> > > and a kepi on his head
> > > always hard at work

To perceive
> > the history of birds
> > I had to see
> > the red-and-blue bird
> > too large for that forest
> > precariously perched on a branch
> > > like a phantom
> > > (swaying in the breeze)

one had to see the bird
in that silence
made of small vegetal sounds
And the bird—creating its history—flew away
not knowing why
and perched on another tree
first almost hidden
then resembling a flower, then a colorful leaf,
and then disappeared

The history of vultures
is nearly the same as the history of owners
of dogs that die
run over
at their front door,
those who have parrots that learn to talk
in the kitchen
and finches
that sing
in a barbershop birdcage

(the barber's daughter
ran away with the mailman's
son, a dark-skinned
postal clerk.
The neighborhood ladies gossiped,
"If she'd run off
with a white man
she could've gotten married")

Through all this
Dr. Gonçalves Moreira (on Beira Mar Avenue
at the entrance to the bay) kept a pair

of Belgian canaries in a silver cage
in his living room
And he brought an Indian girl
from her home in Barra do Corda
to clean his house (white
linen sheets smelling of lavender)
and look after the canaries:
she cleaned out the cage
and changed the water and seed
every morning
at the porch window
(during the war)
Down in the backyard
the washerwoman scrubbed clothes
in a washtub

   and sang along with the water
   The papaya tree next to the wall
   ripened fruit for the doctor's dessert
     (this was around 1942 or '43,
     when the Americans arrived
     to build the Tirirical Army Air Base—
     they bought all the fruits and vegetables
     in the market,
     paid Antônio José an incredible salary,
     and put their feet up on the table
     in the Moto Bar)
       And the canaries, with a shrug of
           indifference,
      would sing in their silver cage

      Camélia became a whore
      As the pill didn't yet exist

she paid more and more
for the uncomfortable love she
made behind the clothesline
leaning against the fence
while her family slept
under the mint-scented air,
the scent of birthday candies.
Her father, Senhor Cunha, a barber,
was nearly shamed to death,
he who shaved the beards
of all the men on their street
(the finch in the cage
shrugged with indifference)
Why does a man have daughters?
And three, for Christ's sake
The oldest, who was the most clever,
went to Josias for
an injection of eucalyptus extract
and the male nurse warned her:
"It's very painful. It's better in a place
with more flesh"
And since that holy day
she had an injection every afternoon
(and the finch
shrugged with indifference)
The third one turned solemn

and took vows as a Daughter of Mary
(and the finch
shrugged with indifference)
The yellow finch
stopped singing when
one Sunday morning

Senhor Neco killed his wife
who—they say—put horns on him:
the cage rolled on the floor
("He stabbed her in the back,
right here he knifed her, in the back.
She didn't lose a drop of blood,
the bleeding was internal.")
Death spread over the streets,
moved among the orchard trees,
pervaded the kitchen of our house
reached the smell of meat roasting in the pan
glistened on the dinnerware
set on the table
for lunch

Hooray for the woman in cream
Put the slipper on the one in green
But a woman in her calico
Will always keep her man in tow

But this is the story of birds
urbanhumanized from a long time ago
and only warriors know
only they understand
the story of the birds
when the wind
blows it through the trees of São Luís
(in a recollection)

It wouldn't be right to say
that Newton Ferreira's life
slipped by or was spent
among baskets of shrimp, bags of rice,
and bushels of manioc flour
in his market
on the corner of Afogados
and Alegria Street.
                    It wouldn't be right because
if you dropped by
around three in the afternoon (a
tranquil hour)—my father leaning on
the countertop reading X-9 comic books—
you would see that everything was fixed
in the same white stillness
of the corn in the bin
and the shelves stacked with cans and bottles
and the countertop with the Filizola scale
                              everything
on the green-and-white mosaic floor
like a stage for the afternoon
Fixed and at the same time thrust
into an ample system
                    that included the warehouses
of Praia Grande, the São Luís–Teresina Railroad,
ranches in Coroatá, Codó, plantations of rice
and tobacco, workers who scatter shrimp to dry
in the sun in Guimarães, and even the families
in the street
who would later sit around the dinner table
For this very reason
he could dive into a world of American gangsters
without concern

It's true, however, that one block up the street
(at his back)
on Gomes de Castro Avenue
the afternoon passed noisily
chattering in the oitizeiro trees as if wind through a clock of leaves

The afternoon has many speeds
                              being slower
for example
when it tears apart a bull-shaped cloud
that it drags away glowing
                              in the direction of Desterro
above the capital
(like a spider, you might say?
that draws in its prey to feed on it?
or like an invisible vulture that eviscerates the cloud
                        in an aerial
                        ballet,
high above the roof of the market?)
And as part of yet another system
                                    this one made
                                    of winds
                                    sometimes with rain
advances darkly from the banks of the Apeadouro,
or from the headwaters of the Bacanga,
a gale that upsets aircraft

No,
to speak of spiders isn't right
if I'm thinking of the city unfolding in its
tile roofs and church towers
                              beneath a searing sun

the families beneath roof tiles, photo portraits of the dead
with faces colored in too brightly,
set in gilded frames,
                           antique
chests of drawers, small boxes full of buttons and balls of linen thread,
tubercular relatives in darkened rooms, coughing
softly so the neighbors won't hear, children
                                   just beginning to walk
clinging to the legs of helpless parents,
         beneath those dingy red-tile roofs
           of our small city
                 that
                 someone flying in from the USA
                 can see
                 between the dirty mouths of two rivers
                 down below
                 looking like forever. But
                 the orchard on Cajazeiras Street? The Shits and Bones
Cistern? The Bishop's Fountain? Newton Ferreira's
                 grocery store?
                           The hypothetical Braniff
                 passenger flying so high
                 cannot see any of these things

                           Leaning on the countertop
                           Newton Ferreira reads his
                           detective stories
                           He knows nothing of the meteorological
           conspiracies plotted
in the lofty spheres above the Atlantic
           In his grocery store
           time doesn't flow

but instead piles up
in bars of Martins soap
slabs of dried beef
bacon all the merchandise
with its prices and
its smells
marked at retail
      (kerosene's
      dirty eye
      spies from the can under the countertop)
      But one sees none of this
flying above the city at 600 miles per hour

      Not even by walking
between those two rows of one-door-and-a-window houses,
two-window homes with iron balconies and friezes
      mottled with dry rot
        (in the red
      afternoon)
        Not even if the grocery
is still there and it's now eight in the evening
and you might see
the light through the single half-opened door
      as before
and there might be men conversing inside
      between swigs of sugarcane liquor
      and though the countertop
      and smell of the merchandise might be the same
you won't find Gonzaga, the army marching-band sergeant
They'll no longer speak of the war since the war ended
      years ago.

Going up or down the street
even if on foot
you'll see the houses are practically the same
but unfamiliar faces
will loom in the windows
as if from a nightmare.

Leaving home was
an apprenticeship to death: my
room with its damp and moldy walls
the backyard in the rain
overgrown with vegetation
and the kitchen
and the lamp cord covered with flies
our home
full of our voices
now has other dwellers:
you're still alive and you see, and you see
that you didn't need to be here to see
The houses, the cities,
are just places through which
we pass through
in passing by

(either sitting or sleeping
or eating at the table
drinking water from the jar
or leaning
on the windowsill, the moist
chicken dripping beneath
the trellised plants)

Neither by standing still, nor crawling,
nor by pressing your ear to the ground
will you ever hear again what was said there
                    But the kerosene, yes,
        you can still smell it on the rags,
                    and soap, perhaps,
            if the factory hasn't shut down
                    But of Newton Ferreira, ex–
center forward of the Maranhão team,
                    known to everyone downtown,
            and who went bust ten times,
                    no trace remains
    on the green-and-white mosaic floor
                    (you'll also search in vain
                    in tonight's B-movie feature)

Still, from up high you can see the city almost unchanged
                    with its streets and plazas
                    where he walked

Oh, my green city

        my humid city

        eternally beaten by many winds

rustling your days at the entrance to the sea

        my sonorous city

        spheres of heavy winds

rolling crazy above the belvederes

        across the soccer fields

        green green green green

        oh rustling shadows

        I drag through other streets

        Lightning from your waters penetrates

my body deeply,

        penetrates so deeply and completely

        and it seems that I'm so small

for the many lives and deaths and lives

            unfolding

in the darkness of clarities

            in the nape of my neck

in my elbow, in the roof of my mouth

in the tomb of my mouth

            stage of unexpected

resurrections

        (my songbird

        city)

        of darkness maybe yours maybe mine

        I no longer know

but in some part of the body (of your body? of

            mine?)

        glitters

        jasmine

though dirtied from the scarcity of surrounding joy
in the empty street
full of leaves and shadows

Waste water rushes down
through your sewers
dragging me in coat and tie
I rise up in your mirrors
I see myself in ancient faces
I see you in my many faces
possessed lost fractured
reflected
unreflected
and the red daisies
drooping over the cistern edge:
the lightning of your waters
penetrates deeply in a
vertigo of white voices milky echoes
of warm saliva on my prick
body seeking body
In the pasture hidden
in the grass its protection and affection
like a horse sniffing
the smell of the earth the green
smell of the forest the pungency of the new smell
of the forest new with life
life of green
things growing
far from that furniture where only the past is alive
far from the world of death of sickness of shame
of the outrage of bill collectors at the door
there

drinking the health of the earth and of plants

                                         seeking

within me the source of a joy

however filthy and furtive

the warm saliva the delight

of one's own body on his body

with earthborne movement

in the grass

heavenly is the cock rising in flight

                                      and falling

Oh, my dirty city

you suffer deeply and in silence

                  from the shame the family smothers

                  in its deepest drawers

                  of faded dresses

                  of tattered shirts

                  of legions of degraded people

                  barely eating

yet embroidering flowers on

                  their tablecloths on

                  their table centerpieces

with water jars

                  —in the afternoon

                  throughout the afternoon

                  throughout their life—

                          filled with

                          crepe paper flowers

                          covered in dust

my aching city

I'm reflected in your
gathered waters:
           in the glass
of water
in the bottle of water
in the barrel of water
in the bathtub naked in the bathroom
dressed in the clothes
of your waters
that undress me and descend
diligently toward the sewer grate
as if they knew beforehand
where to go
         Where
did they go those waters of
so many afternoon baths?
We flow with those afternoons
         into the sewer grate
and now
I flow
into the abyss of smells
that burst into my flesh
into yours, city
you poison me with your presence
you drag me through darkness
you stun me with jasmine
you wet me with saliva and thrust me
into a tightened
         asshole you make me
delirious you smear me
with shit and my dream blows up
in shit

On the city gardens
I piss pus. I wander
on Estrela Street, I slide
down Precipício Lane
I bathe in the Ribeirão
I piss in the Bishop's Fountain
I lose my sight on Sol Street
on Paz Street I revolt
I spurn myself on Comércio
but on Hortas I bloom
on Prazeres I sob
on Palma I greet myself

        on Alecrim I smell good
        on Saúde I feel sick
        on Desterro I run into myself
        on Alegria I get lost
        on Carmo Street I wail
        on Direita I transgress
        and on Aurora I fall asleep

I wake up in the tenderloin. The day howls, it sails
        puffed up and blue
                I fly
with white towels
        I alight on Isabel's smile
I trip on a bias I fall from the clouds
                I discover Marília
I snuggle in her petals like the Divine
dove among roses on a tray
        But June arrives and stabs me
        July arrives and tears me
        September displays my mortal remains

on the city's posts
(later I retrieve myself
sew the pieces together, but my bowels
will never be the same)
I preach subversion of poetic
order, and they pay me. I preach
subversion of political order,
and they hang me near the English tennis courts
on Beira Mar Avenue
                              (and the canaries,
with a shrug of indifference, improvise
on their silver flutes)

I sell what I own and move
to the nation's capital

(If I had married Maria de Lourdes,
some of my children would have been golden, others
dark with green eyes
and I'd have been elected to the House and a member
of the Maranhão Academy of Letters;
if I had married Marília,
I'd have killed myself surrounded by the records of Radio Timbira)

But in the city there was
so much light
                  life
made the century turn in the clouds
                                        above our veranda
above me and the chickens in the backyard
                                        above
the storeroom where

flour barrels jeered
        in the back of the store
               and it meant little
to live, even
in the billiards hall, even
in Castro's bar, in Maroca's
boardinghouse on Saturday nights, it meant little
        to take a bath and walk down
to the city in the afternoon
(beneath the rustle of the trees)
           there
           in the north of Brazil
           dressed in coarse cotton.

        And being worth so little
        meant a lot,
              for a lot of inconsequence
           was the green
fire of the grass, the moss on the wall, the rooster
that will die one day
the plates in the cabinet
the preserves in the jars, the lack
of affection, the search
for love in things
        Not in people:
in things, in the mute flesh
of things, in the flower's cunt, in the occult
speech of lonely waters:
           for life
was passing over us,
        riding in a jet.

Sunday doesn't have the same speed
                        as Friday's flurry of shopping
                        traffic jams and drinking the
                        icy juice of sugarcane,
                                        nor is there
                        the same speed in
                        the Easter lily and the tide
with its army of bubbles and burning caravels
                        invading the river
                        with a sullen torpor so unlike twilight
                        milling
                        the light from above
with its vast scattered gears.
                        Seated on the floor of her room, Bizuza has
another speed
                        folding the clean and ironed sheets
                        arranging them with the linens, as
                              if life would never end.
                                        And it was
                        in her universe of lunches and seasonings
                        of bay leaves and black pepper
                        wild mustard for a stubborn cough,
                                      a universe
of pans and fatigue between the walls of the kitchen
                        where she wore a threadbare cotton print
                        dress,
and her tiny heart beat.
                      And if life wasn't eternal,
inside and outside the cupboard
it is certain that
everything possessing its own speed

(the dark speed
of molasses, the bright
speed of splashing
water)
each thing withdrew
unequally
from its possible eternity.
                        Or
                        if you wish
                        would weave it
                        unequally
in its own light or dark flesh
in a current more profound than the hours of the week.
                        That's why it's a mistake to say
you can see the city better
                        on Sunday
—the tile façades, Sol Street empty
the windows barred in silence—
                        when
                        perfectly still
                        it appears to waver.

And how much better you can see a city
            when—as with Alcântara—
            all its inhabitants have left
and nothing remains (not even
            a dresser mirror in one of those
            roofless houses) only
                        the persistent certainty
                        among the ruins that
                        on the ground
                        where brush now grows

they actually danced
(and you can almost hear voices
and bursts of laughter
      rising and falling in the folds of the wind).
                                              But

      if it's frightening to think
how so much disappeared, so many
wardrobes and beds and servant girls
so many skirts, slips,
shoes of every description
carried off by the wind, away with the clouds,
                            the morning
answers to this
with its many blue speeds
keeps moving
      with joy in oblivion.

                    It's impossible to say
        at how many different speeds
                    a city moves
                                    at each moment
                                    (not counting the dead
                                    who fly backward)
                                    or even a house
        where a kitchen's speed
        differs from a living room's (seemingly still
        with its porcelain vases and knickknacks)
                        or from the backyard
                        open wide to the seasonal gales

                                    and what do you say about
        traffic congestion and the circulation of money
        and goods
                        unequal among classes and neighborhoods, and
                        about the
                        rotation of capital
                        slower among the vegetables
                        quicker in industry, and
        the rotation of sleep
                        under the skin,
                        of dreams
                        in the hair?

                        and the numerous states of water in vessels
                        (about to disappear)
                                        the rotation
                        of the hand searching in pubic hair
                        the wet dream the body's
                        many lips

opening like a rose when caressed, the hand
still there, taking on
the scents of a woman
                and the rotation
of the other smells
produced on the farm
together with the resin of trees and the songs
of birds?

                What do you say about the circulation
                of solar light
inching through the dust under the wardrobe
            among the shoes?
                                and of the circulation
            of cats in the house
            of doves on the breeze?
each of these moving with its very own speed
            and the speed itself
            each thing bears within
                    as with a pear's
            systems of sugar and alcohol
                    cycling
            with different rhythms
                            (you can
            almost hear them)
                            composing the overall speed
            of a pear

in the same way that all these speeds
        compose
(our face reflected in the water tank)
        the day

that passes
—or passed—
in São Luís

And in the same way
that there are many speeds in a
single day
and within a single day there are many days,
you cannot
say that the day
has a single center
(like the pit of a fruit
or a sun)
for in truth
the center of a day is everywhere
like, say, in a water jug
in a dining room
or in a kitchen
where a family
moves at random

And if in this instance
thirst is the force of gravity
other metabolic functions
create other centers
like the latrine and
the bed
or the dining room table
(under a sooty lamp in a
simple home on Alegria Street
during the war)
not to mention the civic centers, the spiritualist

                    centers, the Gonçalves Dias
Cultural Center, or the fish markets,
                    schools, churches, and brothels
                    and the many other centers of the system
                    that the day moves around
(always with a different speed)
                    without ever leaving its place

                    Because
                    when all those suns go out
                    the empty city will remain
                         (like Alcântara)
                         in the same place

Because
unlike the solar system
                    it is not the sun that sustains
                    these systems but
the various bodies
revolving in them:
not the table but hunger
sustains them,
not the bed but fatigue
sustains them,
not the bank but unpaid labor
sustains them

And this is why
when people leave
                    (as they have from Alcântara)
the suns go out (the

pots, the stoves)
their sources of warmth extinguished
This is why
in São Luís
where the people stayed
the city still moves at this moment
in its many systems
and speeds
so that when a jug breaks
another jug is made
another bed is made
another pitcher is made
another man
is made
so the fire
in the kitchen stove
doesn't go out

What they said in the kitchen
                              or on the porch of the house
                              (on Sol Street)
                              flew out the windows

                              it was heard in the downstairs rooms
of the neighbors' house, in the back of the furniture store
                              (and who knows
                              how many things are said in a city
                              how many voices
                              slip through that intricate labyrinth
                              of walls, rooms, and courtyards
                              of bathrooms, of patios, of backyards
                                                          voices
                              among walls and plants
                                                  laughter
                              that lasts a moment and then goes out)

                              And words are living things
that tremble with the joy of the body that shouts them,
each with its own perfume, the taste
          of flesh
that is never really given
even in bed
                              unless to oneself
                              to one's own vertigo
                                                  or likewise
                                                  talking
                                                  or laughing
                                                  within the family circle

while like a mouse
you can hear and see
from your hole
how those voices bounce against the walls of the empty patio
on the iron grating where a grapevine dries
on wires
in the afternoon
          in a small Latin American city

And in them there is
a mortal illumination
                    born in the mouth
                    in no particular time
but which there
in our house
                    filled with cheap furniture
                    and no exceptional dignity
sapped our very existence.

                                        We laughed, it's true,
around the birthday table covered with mint candies
wrapped in colored tissue paper,
                              sure, we laughed,
but
it was as if no affection was enough
as if it made no sense to laugh
                         in such a little city

The man is in the city
as a thing is in another city
and the city is in the man
who is in another city

but there are many ways
an object
can hold another:
the man, you see, isn't in the city
as a tree
is in another city
nor as a tree
is in any one of its leaves
(even fluttering far from it)
The man isn't in the city
as a tree is in a book
when a gust of wind turns its leaves

the city's in the man
but not in the way
a bird is in a tree
not in the way that a bird
(its image)
is/was in the water
nor in the way
the bird's fear
is in the bird I write about

the city's in the man
the way a tree flies
in the bird that leaves it

everything is in another
as its own
and different way
of being in itself

the city's not in the man
as the city's in these
plazas streets and trees

Buenos Aires
May–October 1975